THE SONGS OF ANDREW LLOYD WEBBER™
40 OF HIS GREATEST HITS

Note: the keys in this book do not match the other wind instruments

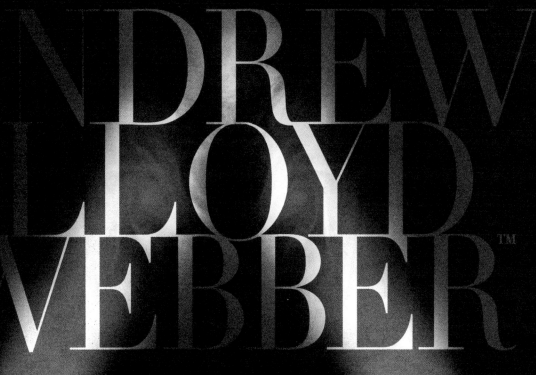

Andrew Lloyd Webber™ is a trademark owned by Andrew Lloyd Webber.

ISBN 978-1-4768-1403-2

HAL•LEONARD®

7777 W. BLUEMOUND RD. P.O. BOX 13819 MILWAUKEE, WI 53213

In Australia Contact:
Hal Leonard Australia Pty. Ltd.
4 Lentara Court
Cheltenham, Victoria, 3192 Australia
Email: ausadmin@halleonard.com.au

Visit Hal Leonard Online at
www.halleonard.com

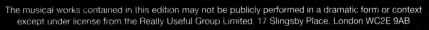

CONTENTS

ALL I ASK OF YOU

from THE PHANTOM OF THE OPERA

HORN

Music by ANDREW LLOYD WEBBER
Lyrics by CHARLES HART
Additional Lyrics by RICHARD STILGOE

ANOTHER SUITCASE IN ANOTHER HALL

from EVITA

Horn

Words by TIM RICE
Music by ANDREW LLOYD WEBBER

Slowly (8 beat feel)

AMIGOS PARA SIEMPRE
(Friends for Life)
(The Official Theme of the Barcelona 1992 Games)

HORN

Music by ANDREW LLOYD WEBBER
Lyrics by DON BLACK

Gently

(small notes optional)

ANGEL OF MUSIC

from THE PHANTOM OF THE OPERA

HORN

Music by ANDREW LLOYD WEBBER
Lyrics by CHARLES HART
Additional Lyrics by RICHARD STILGOE

9

Slower

ANY DREAM WILL DO
from JOSEPH AND THE AMAZING TECHNICOLOR® DREAMCOAT

Horn

Music by ANDREW LLOYD WEBBER
Lyrics by TIM RICE

AS IF WE NEVER SAID GOODBYE
from SUNSET BOULEVARD

Horn

Music by ANDREW LLOYD WEBBER
Lyrics by DON BLACK and CHRISTOPHER HAMPTON,
with contributions by AMY POWERS

CLOSE EVERY DOOR
from JOSEPH AND THE AMAZING TECHNICOLOR® DREAMCOAT

HORN

Music by ANDREW LLOYD WEBBER
Lyrics by TIM RICE

DON'T CRY FOR ME ARGENTINA

from EVITA

Words by TIM RICE
Music by ANDREW LLOYD WEBBER

Horn

EVERYTHING'S ALRIGHT

from JESUS CHRIST SUPERSTAR

Horn

Words by TIM RICE
Music by ANDREW LLOYD WEBBER

I DON'T KNOW HOW TO LOVE HIM

from JESUS CHRIST SUPERSTAR

Horn

Words by TIM RICE
Music by ANDREW LLOYD WEBBER

HIGH FLYING, ADORED

from EVITA

Horn

Words by TIM RICE
Music by ANDREW LLOYD WEBBER

I AM THE STARLIGHT

from STARLIGHT EXPRESS

Horn

Music by ANDREW LLOYD WEBBER
Lyrics by RICHARD STILGOE

I BELIEVE MY HEART

from THE WOMAN IN WHITE

Horn

Music by ANDREW LLOYD WEBBER
Lyrics by DAVID ZIPPEL

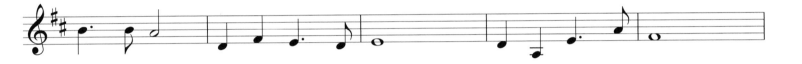

I'M HOPELESS WHEN IT COMES TO YOU

from STEPHEN WARD

HORN

Music by ANDREW LLOYD WEBBER
Book and Lyrics by DON BLACK
and CHRISTOPHER HAMPTON

LEARN TO BE LONELY
from THE PHANTOM OF THE OPERA

HORN

Music by ANDREW LLOYD WEBBER
Lyrics by CHARLES HART

LIGHT AT THE END OF THE TUNNEL

from STARLIGHT EXPRESS

Horn

Music by ANDREW LLOYD WEBBER
Lyrics by RICHARD STILGOE

LOVE CHANGES EVERYTHING

from ASPECTS OF LOVE

Horn

Music by ANDREW LLOYD WEBBER
Lyrics by DON BLACK and CHARLES HART

(small notes optional)

MEMORY
from CATS

Horn

Music by ANDREW LLOYD WEBBER
Text by TREVOR NUNN after T.S. ELIOT

LOVE NEVER DIES

from LOVE NEVER DIES

HORN

Music by ANDREW LLOYD WEBBER
Lyrics by GLENN SLATER

(small note optional)

MAKE UP MY HEART

from STARLIGHT EXPRESS

Horn

Music by ANDREW LLOYD WEBBER
Lyrics by RICHARD STILGOE

MR. MISTOFFELEES

from CATS

Horn

Music by ANDREW LLOYD WEBBER
Text by T.S. ELIOT

THE MUSIC OF THE NIGHT
from THE PHANTOM OF THE OPERA

HORN

Music by ANDREW LLOYD WEBBER
Lyrics by CHARLES HART
Additional Lyrics by RICHARD STILGOE

NO MATTER WHAT

from WHISTLE DOWN THE WIND

Horn

Music by ANDREW LLOYD WEBBER
Lyrics by JIM STEINMAN

THE PERFECT YEAR

from SUNSET BOULEVARD

HORN

Music by ANDREW LLOYD WEBBER
Lyrics by DON BLACK
and CHRISTOPHER HAMPTON

THE PHANTOM OF THE OPERA
from THE PHANTOM OF THE OPERA

Horn

Music by ANDREW LLOYD WEBBER
Lyrics by CHARLES HART
Additional Lyrics by RICHARD STILGOE
and MIKE BATT

Moderately fast

PIE JESU
from REQUIEM

HORN

By ANDREW LLOYD WEBBER

STARLIGHT EXPRESS

from STARLIGHT EXPRESS

Horn

Music by ANDREW LLOYD WEBBER
Lyrics by RICHARD STILGOE

THE POINT OF NO RETURN
from THE PHANTOM OF THE OPERA

HORN

Music by ANDREW LLOYD WEBBER
Lyrics by CHARLES HART
Additional Lyrics by RICHARD STILGOE

(small notes optional)

Moderately

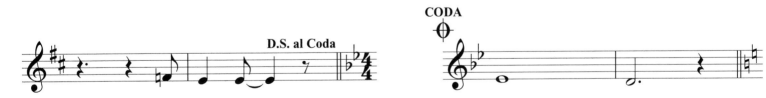

SEEING IS BELIEVING

from ASPECTS OF LOVE

Horn

Music by ANDREW LLOYD WEBBER
Lyrics by DON BLACK and CHARLES HART

(small notes optional)

STICK IT TO THE MAN
from SCHOOL OF ROCK

HORN

Music by ANDREW LLOYD WEBBER
Lyrics by GLENN SLATER

SUPERSTAR
from JESUS CHRIST SUPERSTAR

HORN

Words by TIM RICE
Music by ANDREW LLOYD WEBBER

TELL ME ON A SUNDAY
from SONG & DANCE

Horn

Music by ANDREW LLOYD WEBBER
Lyrics by DON BLACK

TAKE THAT LOOK OFF YOUR FACE

from SONG & DANCE

HORN

Music by ANDREW LLOYD WEBBER
Lyrics by DON BLACK

Moderately

THINK OF ME
from THE PHANTOM OF THE OPERA

Horn

Music by ANDREW LLOYD WEBBER
Lyrics by CHARLES HART
Additional Lyrics by RICHARD STILGOE

'TIL I HEAR YOU SING

from LOVE NEVER DIES

Music by ANDREW LLOYD WEBBER
Lyrics by GLENN SLATER

HORN

(small notes optional)

UNEXPECTED SONG

from SONG & DANCE

HORN

Music by ANDREW LLOYD WEBBER
Lyrics by DON BLACK

(small notes optional)

WHISTLE DOWN THE WIND

from WHISTLE DOWN THE WIND

Horn

Music by ANDREW LLOYD WEBBER
Lyrics by JIM STEINMAN

WISHING YOU WERE SOMEHOW HERE AGAIN

from THE PHANTOM OF THE OPERA

HORN

Music by ANDREW LLOYD WEBBER
Lyrics by CHARLES HART
Additional Lyrics by RICHARD STILGOE

Moderately slow

(small notes optional)

WITH ONE LOOK

from SUNSET BOULEVARD

Horn

Music by ANDREW LLOYD WEBBER
Lyrics by DON BLACK and CHRISTOPHER HAMPTON,
with contributions by AMY POWERS

Moderately slow

To Coda

D.C. al Coda

CODA

YOU MUST LOVE ME
from the Cinergi Motion Picture EVITA

Words by TIM RICE
Music by ANDREW LLOYD WEBBER

HORN